Christa McAul

NASA (National Aeronautics and Space Administration) wanted to send a teacher into space. Sharon Christa McAuliffe was the first teacher to be chosen. Christa didn't want to be an astronaut though. She wanted to teach children about space.

Christa with some of her students

In 1948 Christa McAuliffe was born in Framingham, Massachusetts. As a young girl, she loved school, music lessons, Girl Scouts, and sports. She wanted to be a teacher when she grew up.

As an adult, Christa taught social studies to high-school students.

Christa studied to be a teacher. She married her husband, Steven, just after she finished college.

Christa and Steven
with their children,
Scott and Caroline

After college Christa's life was busy raising two children and teaching social studies at a high school in New Hampshire. She believed that each student learned best by doing activities and seeing things in person.

Christa's excitement in her classroom carried over to her training.

Then Christa heard about a search for a teacher to go into space. Steve told Christa to "go for it." Those words changed both their lives.

Christa told her students any dream could come true if they had the courage to work at it.

In order to be chosen, teachers had to tell why they wanted to go into space. Christa didn't apply until just before the deadline.

One of ten finalists, McAuliffe smiles as Vice President George Bush tells her she has been selected.

Many of the teachers who applied for the contest wanted to teach science projects. Christa wanted to keep a journal of her training and record her thoughts. Then she could share her flight with her students. This simple idea helped NASA to choose Christa McAuliffe.

Other teachers congratulate Christa.

NASA chose Sharon Christa McAuliffe on July 19, 1985. She would be the first teacher to travel into space.

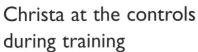
Christa at the controls during training

Christa, with Steve, proudly shows her space suit.

Christa had to learn to do simple things in different ways. On Earth gravity pulls us down. In space there is no gravity. Everything can float away. Christa had to learn to eat, sleep, and move in space.

Christa trained every day.

10–9–8–7–6–5–4–3–2–1 Blast off! The rocket that carried the space shuttle *Challenger* was launched on January 28, 1986. Just minutes into the flight, the space shuttle exploded. Christa and all of the astronauts died in the explosion.

The *Challenger* crew:
Front—Michael J. Smith, Francis R. (Dick)
  Scobee, Ronald E. McNair
Back—Ellison S. Onizuka, Sharon Christa
  McAuliffe, Gregory Jarvis, Judith A. Resnick

Christa had dreamed of being a teacher. She is remembered and honored as the first teacher in space.

Christa will be remembered as a person who tried hard and did the best she could.

Let's Explore!

Christa McAuliffe was born in Massachusetts. She taught school in New Hampshire. She trained for her space flight in Texas. She took off on her flight from Florida. Find on the map the cities in which these events happened.

What Do You Think?

My Journal

Christa McAuliffe wanted to keep a journal about her space flight. Keep a journal for a week. Write about what you learn and do during that week.

Planet Mobile

The planets are different sizes. They circle the sun. Color and cut out a circle to stand for each planet. Create a planet mobile with the sun in the center.

Space Report

Choose a "space" topic such as planets, the sun, or the moon. Find out about it in books or an encyclopedia. Share this information with a friend.

THE SPACE SHUTTLE

Look at these photos and diagrams. The space shuttle is big. The shuttle has three levels. Look at where the astronauts sleep.

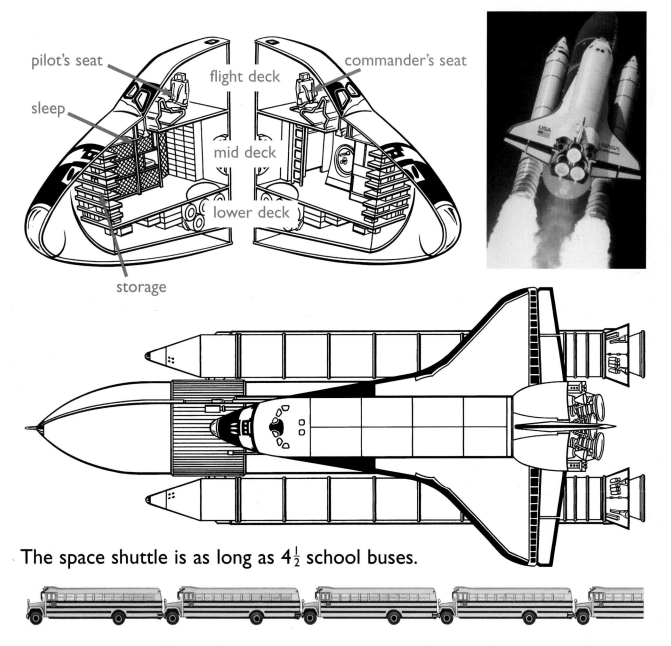

pilot's seat

flight deck

commander's seat

sleep

mid deck

lower deck

storage

The space shuttle is as long as $4\frac{1}{2}$ school buses.

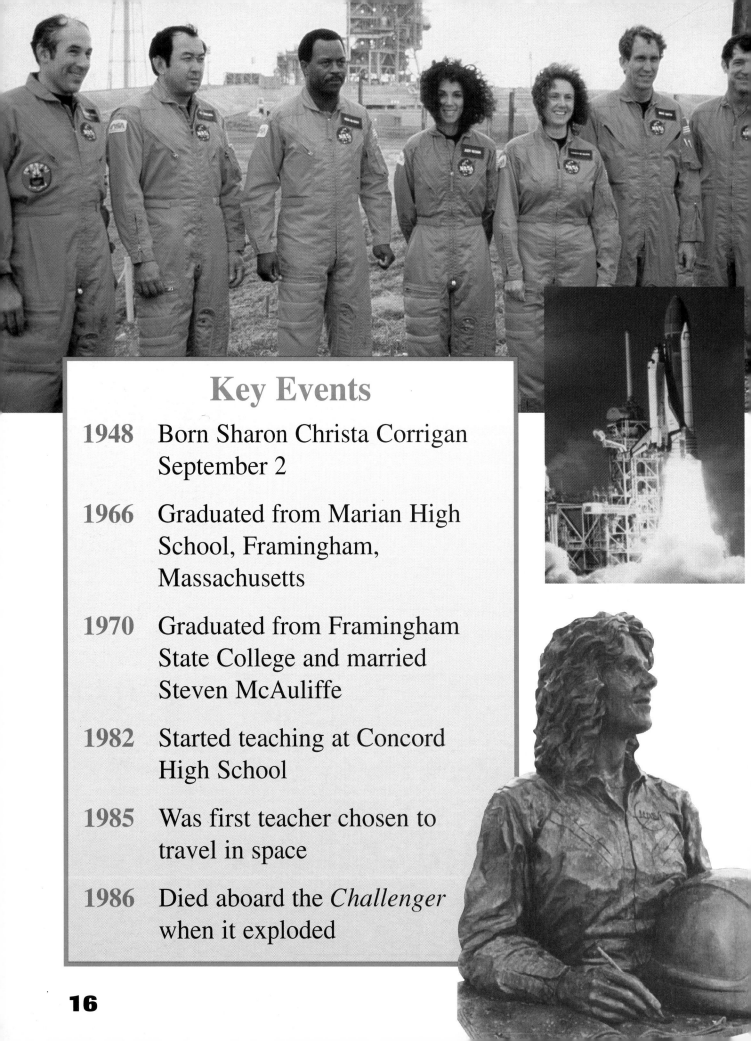

Key Events

1948 Born Sharon Christa Corrigan September 2

1966 Graduated from Marian High School, Framingham, Massachusetts

1970 Graduated from Framingham State College and married Steven McAuliffe

1982 Started teaching at Concord High School

1985 Was first teacher chosen to travel in space

1986 Died aboard the *Challenger* when it exploded